MIKE TH

HEROINES OF THE BIBLE
GOD'S FAIR LADIES

5 FUN BIBLE STORIES

BY MIKE THALER
ILLUSTRATIONS BY DENNIS ADLER

Equipping Kids for Life!
faithkids.com

A Faith Building Guide can be found on page 32.

Dedicated to
Don, Karen, and Sarah Callen
our family of friends.
Mike

Faith Kids® is an imprint of
Cook Communications, Colorado Springs, Colorado 80918
Cook Communications, Paris, Ontario
Kingsway Communications, Eastbourne, England

HEROINES OF THE BIBLE
© 2002 by Mike Thaler for text and Dennis Adler for illustrations

All rights reserved. Except for brief excerpts for review purposes,
no part of this book may be reproduced or used in any form
without written permission from the publisher.

Faith Kids® is a registered trademark of Cook Communications Ministries.

Published in association with the literary agency of Alive Communications, Inc.,
7680 Goddard St., Suite 200, Colorado Springs CO 80920.

Edited by Heather Gemmen
Designed by Clyde Van Cleve

First printing, 2002
Printed in Singapore
06 05 04 03 02   5 4 3 2 1

Library of Congress Cataloging-in-Publication

Thaler, Mike, 1936-
  Heroines of the Bible : God's fair ladies / by Mike Thaler ; illustrated by Dennis Adler.
    p. cm. --
  Summary: Five comical retellings of Bible stories demonstrate how God values women.
  ISBN 0-7814-3651-6
    1. Bible stories, English--O.T. 2. Bible. O.T. --Juvenile humor. [1. Women in the Bible
  2. Bible stories--O.T.] I. Adler, Dennis (Dennis H.), 1942- ill. II. Title.

BS551.3 .T474 2002
221.9'22'082--dc21

2001055677

"Mike Thaler is proof positive that the funny bone is connected to the learning bone."
— Emmett Cooper, Ph.D
President, HoneyWord® Way of Learning

Mike Thaler Presents . . .

- Action Heroes of the Bible: The Sermonators
- Prophets of the Bible: God's Anchormen
- Heroines of the Bible: God's Fair Ladies

Books in the Heaven and Mirth® Series:

- Adam and the Apple Turnover
- Moses: Take Two Tablets and Call Me in the Morning
- The Prodigal Son: Oh Brother
- Daniel: Nice Kitty!
- David & Bubblebath Sheba
- David: God's Rock Star
- Elijah: Prophet Sharing
- John the Baptist, Wet & Wild
- Paul: God's Message Sent Apostle Post

"A romping fun read-aloud for kids (and grown-ups who still like to grin)."
— Becky Freeman
Best-selling author and speaker

"Out loud! Out loud! This book must be read out loud! Why? Because that's the way that kids will laugh—OUT LOUD! That's the way that parents will laugh! And everyone will learn because laughter lubricates learning."
— Calvin Miller
Best-selling author and speaker

Rahab and the Spies Give Us a Break

WHEN JOSHUA WAS GETTING READY
to attack Jericho, he sent two spies
into town to scope out the scene—
double oy seven and *double oy eight*.
They put on their camel disguise,
trotted into town,
and stopped at
Rahab's Bed and Breakfast
to get a little info.
But the spies of the king
of Jericho, disguised as goats,
spied the spies
whom they despised,
and told the king
who immediately dispatched
a swat team disguised as flies.

They buzzed over to Rahab's.

"We've got you surrounded!"
    they shouted,
    circling the house.
    "Come out
    with your hooves up!"

Rahab hid the camel
    in her closet
    and leaned out the window.
    "You're too late, boys,"
    she shouted.
    "They already cut out.
    They went that-a-way!"
She pointed to the zoo.
So the flies buzzed off
and did a cage-by-cage search.

"Listen," said Rahab to the camel,
"I know you guys are going to
take over this town.
I heard all about you,
and I'm scared.
God's on your side,
and nobody can stand against Him.

But listen, since I helped you,
will you give me
and my family a break?"
"Sure," nodded *double oy seven*,
who was the first hump.
"Tie this red ribbon
in your window,
and you and your family
will be spared."

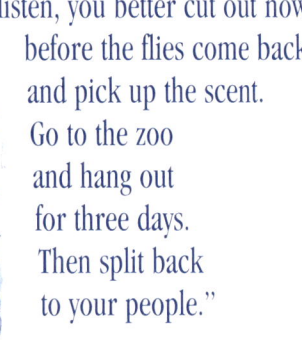

"*Oy*, thank you."
"But listen, you better cut out now
before the flies come back
and pick up the scent.
Go to the zoo
and hang out
for three days.
Then split back
to your people."

So she lowered the camel
out of her window
on a rope,
and the camel galloped to the zoo
where it hung out for three days.
It made friends with a yak
and a penguin
who were also spies in disguises.
After three days it loped back to Joshua.

"They're scared to death of us,"
reported *double oy seven*,
the front hump.

"We got it knocked,"
agreed *double oy eight*,
the back hump.

"Great!" said Joshua.
 "Let's get crackin' with the attackin'.
  And by the way,
   you can take off that
    crazy camel costume now."

So Rahab, who had hung the ribbon
in her window,
and her family were spared.
And that's how Rahab-bilitation came about.*

The End

Nuggets from Goldie, the miner prophet:
"You can even trust a camel when it's working for God."

For the real story, read Joshua 2 and 6:22–25.

* Rahab was later to be inducted into the Hall of Faith. (See Hebrews 11:31.)

Ruth
Momma Mia!

THINGS WERE TOUGH
in Judah. So Elimelon*
took his wife Naomi
and their two sons to Moab
to see if he could find work.
But instead of getting
a steady job,
he died—which is steady,
but without a paycheck.
Naomi, now a single mom,
brought up her two sons,
who then married Moabite women.
But then the two sons died,
leaving the three women
without a breadwinner.

*Son of Watermelon

"You girls start dating again. Go out and have a good time. I'll just sit here and starve," said Naomi.

"No way!" said Orpah and Ruth, her two daughters-in-law.

"I'm going home," wailed Naomi. "You girls go get jobs at Woolworths,* remarry, and have lots of kids."

"Okay," agreed Orpah sheepishly, but she later changed her name to Oprah, joined the opera, and went on TV.

"Why don't you go on TV, too," said Naomi. "You could change your name to Dr. Ruth."

"No way," repeated Ruth. "I'm with you all the way, Mom!" So Naomi and Ruth walked back to Judah. When they arrived, half starved and shabby with sore feet, everyone was glad to see them.

"How are things going?" they asked.

"Not so well," sobbed Naomi.

"How are Elimelon and the boys?"

"All dead," wept Naomi. "Trouble is my middle name."

"Well, have a nice day," smiled everyone, and they left.

* a local mutton ranch

"At least I'm not *ruthless*," sighed Naomi.
"Listen, go to the field owned by Boaz,
my distant relative,
and see what you can pick up."

So Ruth put on a little lipstick,
mascara, and rouge and went into the field.
She picked up Boaz, who liked her so well
he decided to marry her.

"That's great," said Naomi, "but have him
get a complete physical before the wedding."

Except for a bad case of athlete's foot,
Boaz passed his checkup, and they were happily married.

"Things are looking up," smiled Naomi as she moved
into their tent. "I'm not losing a daughter," she joked.
"I'm gaining a pension plan."

The happy couple soon had a son who grew up and had David
(of David and Goliath) who became king of Israel.
And he always had a special place in his heart for his
grandmother Ruth and his great grandmother-in-law Naomi.

THE END

Nuggets from Goldie, the miner prophet:
"The path of righteousness is better than the yellow brick road."

For the real story, read the book of Ruth.

Deborah and Jael
Ladies Win the Day

WHEN THE JEWS WANDERED from worshipping God and turned to worshipping statues of pink flamingos and the seven dwarves,* God grew angry. He allowed Jabin the king of the Canaanites to sweep down on the Israelites with his chariots of iron and conquer them.

Jabin ruled really cruelly for twenty years. These were hard times for the Jews, and they began to realize that things had been better when they worshipped the Lord Almighty. So they cleared all the statues off their lawns and went back to synagogue.

*This is called *Pray* and *Stray*.

At this time the Jews were led
by a judge name Deborah.
Her proud mother called her
"my daughter the judge."
Deborah was very wise.
She'd sit under a palm tree
and people would
bring her their problems
and ask her questions.
She also had a column
in the local paper
called *Dear Debby*.
And people would
write her letters:

Dear Debby,
My husband still worships
lawn furniture. What should I do?

Dear Debby,
What's the difference between a camel
and a dromedary?

Dear Debby,
How can we win against Jabin's chariots of iron
and free ourselves?

Deborah took this last letter seriously
and sent for a man called Barak the Brave.

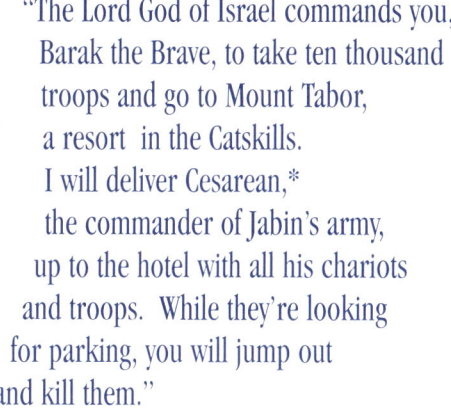

"The Lord God of Israel commands you,
Barak the Brave, to take ten thousand
troops and go to Mount Tabor,
a resort in the Catskills.
I will deliver Cesarean,*
the commander of Jabin's army,
up to the hotel with all his chariots
and troops. While they're looking
for parking, you will jump out
and kill them."

"No way," quivered Barak the Brave.
"Those chariots will run right over us.
We wouldn't stand a chance.
I could even get hurt."

"Stop crying, Barak the Brave.
I'll go with you and hold your hand."

"Okay," sniffled Barak the Brave, drying his eyes,
"if you come with me and hold *both* hands."

"But, Barak the Brave," warned Deborah,
"since you have shown such little faith in the Word of God,
he will turn the capture of Cesarean over to a woman."

"Unlikely," scoffed Barak the Brave, ringing out his hanky.
"Women are sissies. I'll capture Cesarean."

"We'll see," said Debby with a smile.

* Just joking, his name was Sisera.

So they all went up to Mount Tabor
and had a big battle.
The Lord overturned the chariots of iron
and the Israelites slew all the Canaanite troops
except for Cesarean who cut out.
He made it as far as the tent of Jael,
the local Mary Kay® representative.
She met him at the door.

"Come on in, big boy. You look tired.
Did you have a rough day at the battle?"

Cesarean began to cry. "My chariot fell over
and a bunch of guys chased me
and wanted to stick spears in me."

"Oh, poor baby," soothed Jael.
"Why don't you just lie down
and take a nap."

"Okay, but leave the light on."

"Would you like anything else?"

"A big glass of milk
and a chocolate chip cookie."

After he had drunk all his milk
and eaten his cookie, Cesarean fell asleep.
Jael, who was in the Israelite booster club,

quietly snuck in
and hammered a tent peg into his head
giving him "Excedrin® headache #35."
He woke up and died.

Just then Barak the Brave arrived.
"Where is he? I'm ready to capture him."

Jael pointed to Cesarean
nailed to the floor—
and Barak the Brave fainted.
Now the Jews were free to worship
God Almighty, who had delivered them.
The government was turned back over to a man,
'cause everyone knows women are sissies.
Deborah and Jael opened a flower shop
and did quite well supplying wreaths
for all the military funerals.

THE END

Nuggets from Goldie, the miner prophet:
"Sometimes the fair sex is the fairer sex."

For the real story, read Judges 4.

Zelophehad's Daughters
Women's Rights

ZELOPHEHAD
had five daughters:

Mahlah—the oldest

Noah—who cried a lot

Milcah—who took care of the cows

Tirzah—who also cried a lot

And Hoglah—who took care of the pigs.

They were true farmer's daughters.
When their dad kicked the bucket,
the girls went before Moses.

"Our father died in the desert," cried Noah and Tirzah.

"He had no male heir. He had lots of *facial 'air*, but that doesn't count. So it's just us girls," said Mahlah.

"The farm is tied up in probate," sighed Milkah.

"Give it to us so we can continue his line," declared Hoglah.

"Come back tomorrow," said Moses.
"I have to take this case to the *Supreme* Court."

So the girls left and Moses went before God.

"The girls are right," judged God.
**"They should certainly get the farm.
This is the way it works:**

"If a man dies and leaves no son, turn his inheritance over to his daughter.

"If he has no daughter, give his inheritance to his brother.

"If he has no brother— Are you getting this?— give it to his father's brothers.

"If his father has no brothers, give it to the nearest relative in his clan.

"And if there aren't any relatives, give it all to the lawyers."

So the girls got the farm
with an *oink, oink* here,
and a *moo, moo* there,
and a whole new profession got rich.

THE END

Nuggets from Goldie, the miner prophet:
"When you're living with God's will, everyone's a beneficiary."

For the real story, read Numbers 27:1–11.

Queen Esther
Saved by the Belle

ONCE UPON A TIME there was a great king. His name was Xerxes. He ruled over many lands and many peoples. In the third year of his reign he decided to throw a big bash to impress his nobles, ministers, and generals. They all came to the party which lasted for one hundred and eighty days. Towards the end, there was a catered banquet that lasted seven days.

The wine flowed freely
and nobody's golden goblet
was ever empty.
The king, who was
fairly well in his cups,
sent a command
to his beautiful wife,
queen Vashti,
to come over and show off
her incredible crown.
But the queen was
having a party of her own
and was playing pin the tail on the camel,
so she said, "No."

"NO?" roared the king, growing red
to the roots of his beard.

"No," replied the queen.

"NO?" exclaimed the nobles, ministers, and generals.

"No," stammered the king.

"What are you gonna do about it, huh?"
asked all his nobles, ministers, and generals.

"What should I do?" asked the king.

"Just get a new wife!" declared the nobles, ministers, and generals.

"Okay," said the king.

So the most beautiful girls were gathered like flowers
from all over his kingdom and put into a bouquet
from which the king would pick a wife.
All the contestants went to the beauty shop
for twelve months. They had their hair done,
their nails done, their eyes done.
They were oiled, plucked, and pampered
before they were set before the king.
Now the brightest blossom in the bouquet
was Esther. She was very beautiful
and gained much favor around the palace.
Esther pleased the king greatly
and he chose her to be his queen.

But Esther had a secret. She was a real Jewish princess.
Her uncle Mordecai, who had once saved the king's life,
advised her, "Be cool, girl."
So Esther became the queen and the king was very happy.
In order to spend more time at home,
he raised a man named Haman*
to be his chief operating officer,
and all the other nobles bowed before him.
Everyone, that is, except Mordecai.

"Why don't you bow before me?" shouted Haman.

"*Hey, man*," answered Mordecai. "I'm a Jew.
Jews only bow to God."

---

*Not pronounced like *ham'n' eggs*.

This annoyed Haman, who was very insecure,
and he decided to kill Mordecai and all the Jews.
So edicts were sent out calling for the destruction
of every Jewish man, woman, and child
in the kingdom on *Moanday* the thirteenth,
in the twelfth month of Adar.
When Mordecai read the edict
he felt really bad. He put on sack cloth
and ashes and stood in front
of the king's palace and moaned.
When Esther heard her uncle
wailing, she sent out a servant
to ask him what was the matter.
Mordecai told the servant
about the edict and asked Esther
to plead for her people.
So Esther went before the king
and invited him and Haman
to a dinner party. After they had eaten,
she invited them back
the following evening.
This well pleased Haman,
who liked the queen's cooking.
But on the way home he passed Mordecai
who still wouldn't bow down to him—
and he got indigestion.

"You can do one of two things,"
said Zaresh his wife.
"You can take two alka seltzer,
or you can hang Mordecai."

"I'll hang Mordecai," said Haman,
who didn't like medicine.
He went out and built a tall gallows
in his backyard. Now, that night
the king had indigestion too.*
He couldn't sleep, so he had
his record book brought to him.
And in it he came across the chapter
where Mordecai had saved his life.
He summoned Haman and asked him,
"How should I honor a man
who deserves it?"

Haman thought, "Surely he means me."

"Oh, king," smiled Haman.
"Put your finest robe on the man,
place him on your favorite horse,
and lead him through the streets shouting,
'This is how the king honors a man!'"

"Good," said the king.

"Good," said Haman rubbing his hands together.

*Esther cooked with a lot of jalapeños.

"Get Mordecai and do all this for him."

"Mordecai?" gulped Haman.

"Yes, Mordecai!" answered the king.

"But... But... But..."

"No buts about it," said the king. "Get going!"

So Haman got the royal robe
and placed it on Mordecai
and put him on the king's favorite horse
and led him through the streets shouting,
"This is how the king honors a man!"

Needless to say,
his heart wasn't in it,
and when he got home
he took a whole bottle
of alka seltzer.

"Cheer up," advised his wife.
"You still have the queen's
dinner party tonight."
Haman burped.

At dinner the king asked Esther
what favor he could do for her.
Esther threw herself at his feet.
"Spare my people, oh King!" she cried.

"Who threatens them?" thundered the king.

"Pass the salt," said Haman.

"Him!" said Esther, pointing to Haman. Haman spit out a mouthful of peas.

"He has rotten table manners, too," said the king.

So after dinner Haman's head was covered and he was hanged on his own gallows. Amen!

And to add insult to injury,
Mordecai was given his job,
his land, and his wealth.
A new edict was sent out saving the Jews
and was followed with great rejoicing
and a big party called Purim,*
that has lasted until today.

The End

Nuggets from Goldie the miner prophet:
"God makes sure that bad guys have enough rope to hang themselves."

For the real story, read the book of Esther.

*pronounced *poor 'im*

MIKE THALER PRESENTS ...

Life Issue: Sometimes I wonder if God cares about all people the same.
Spiritual Building Block: Acceptance

Gain understanding of God's love to everyone in the following ways:

Think About It:
If you sat in front of the television watching commercials with the volume turned off, wouldn't it be amazing how many different faces you would see: different shapes, different colors, different ages, different genders, different facial expressions.... God made such a huge variety in people because he loves diversity.

Talk About It:
Next time your parents take you out to eat, ask them if you can go to a restaurant that offers ethnic food. Before you go, pull out a map to look up the country where the people would often eat the type of food you are about to enjoy. At the restaurant, talk with your parents about how interesting people in different cultures are.

Try It:
Go to the library and check out cassette tapes or CDs that play various music styles from around the world. While blasting the music through the house, enjoy the diversity of sound. Again, appreciate how God loves so many different kinds of things and people.